Unveiling THE TRUTH

The Never-Ending Story of My Life

MELINDA FELICIANO

Order this book online at www.trafford.com
or email orders@trafford.com

Most Trafford titles are also available at major online book retailers.

Printed in the United States of America.

ISBN: 978-1-4269-9676-4 (sc)
ISBN: 978-1-4269-9677-1 (hc)
ISBN: 978-1-4269-9678-8 (e)

Library of Congress Control Number: 2011917825

Trafford rev. 11/14/2011

 www.trafford.com

North America & international
toll-free: 1 888 232 4444 (USA & Canada)
phone: 250 383 6864 ♦ fax: 812 355 4082

I would like to thank my parents for being supportive of me after all these years. I would like to give a special thanks to my mom who never gave up on me when things became tough. Also, I would like to thank my big brother for always being good to me. You're someone I have always looked up to and always will. No matter where our lives will take us, you're always in my thoughts. And a special thanks for my two little nieces who give me hope and a reason to live. If it wasn't for you I wouldn't care about anything. I will always love you no matter what age you are.

Ain't It Funny

Ain't it funny how things turn out
Didn't expect it the way it did
No one couldn't understand what I'm talking about
I wasn't gonna go down without a fight

No one believes the things I can do
So ain't it funny what happens to me
When I show others the path I took
It makes them realize that I'm for real
When will I catch a break
When it's gonna be my time
How long was it gonna take
Ain't it funny how things twine

I enjoy living my life no matter what
It's like a whirlwind of imagination
Ain't it funny how my life has been arranged
Each day that I been living

Ain't No Man

Ain't no one gonna put me down
Ain't no man gonna hold me down
Who's gonna be there for me
If it wasn't gonna be a man

What man gonna stand by me
Ain't no man who would be
I have nowhere to go
I have no man to take care of me

I have no man who would love me
Ain't no man that knows how
Who's gonna be the one who would stand by me
What man cares enough for me

Where am I gonna find this person
Where am I gonna find you
Ain't no man that would believe in me
So why should I hold on to u any longer

All By Myself 1

Everything that I do
I do it all by my myself
I don't always ask for help
Or ask anyone else

Once I make it on my own
It's easier for me to do things all by myself
When I'm all grown
It will be easier for me to move on without you

It's not as easy as it may seem
Doin' everything all my myself
I just try to do my best to redeem myself
And hold my head up high

All By Myself 2

I try to do everything alone
I try to do everything all by myself
I felt all grown
That I didn't need anyone to tell me what to do

What do you expect from me now
If I had to do everything all by myself
All I wanted was to be accepted by my peers
And not be in their shadow

When you least expect things to happened
It'll happen in one second
When I did things all by myself
It made me realize the type of person I've become

When I tried to do everything all by myself
Everything goes wrong
But when I asked for help
I didn't know where to turn

Baby It's U

Baby it's u who I needed by my side
There's nothing you can do
There's no place to hide

What's important that I can rely on u
Baby it's u who believed in me
That's all I needed to hear from u

You're the one who I could confide in
You're the one who I run to
Baby it's u who knows me better than anyone
That's why I feel so close to u

Tell me something good tonight
Tell me some else to make me feel all right
Baby it's u who came from the light
And not letting me go down without a fight

Go to that place where you dream of
And don't forget where you come from
Baby it's u who never gave up on me
And believe in me in everyway

Come Clean

I think that you should come clean
And confess to everything that you have done
Even though you don't wanna admit it

I'm beginning to realize what you're about
It's better to come clean now before is too late
It's not easy to live without
Without the love that you bring to me today

When will I see you again
When will you come clean
When am I gonna believe what you say
What are the possibilities of changing your mind

You're not gonna get a second chance
You don't deserve one anyways
Come clean now before its too late
That way we don't have to wait any longer

Come On Over

Why don't you come on over to my place
I'll show you what I'm about
It won't be a total disgrace
To be with me any day

Give me a reason for not giving up
When you come on over to my hood
With everything that we went through
I wish that you would see my point

You never let me forget every little thing
With all the possibilities there was
So why don't you come on over for a while
That way we could resolve this without a fight

Since you left not so long ago
You have been inconsistent for a long time
I don't think it would have been a good idea
If you would have come on over earlier that night

Crush

I've been crushed so many times
It's been so long that I stopped counting
It's hard to let it go
But I'm doing my best no matter what

I've had my crushes since the beginning of time
That it was hard to let it go
Even if nothing didn't make sense
I still tried my best to make it work

I miss you so much
That I don't know what to do
I was so crushed
But it didn't stop me from staying close to u

Loving you made me this way
I don't wanna be crushed by you again
There isn't much to say
Than to say goodbye to you for the last time

Deja Vu

Every where I go I see you
Wasn't sure if it's a dream or a deja vu
After weeks it was clear what it really was
But I wanted to make sure before I act on impulse

I go back and forth tryna put the pieces together
Having this deja vu makes me quiver
Even after days later
I still had the shivers

I had these visions of you
Didn't know what it meant
Was it a deja vu
Or was it something else

Help me figure out this vision that I keep seeing
Is like seeing you every where I go
All I wanted to know was it a deja vu
Or something that is unexplained

Don't Let Go

Don't let go to the one person you love
It's not easy to find that special person these days
When you're waitin' for a sign from above
You'll get the answers that you're searchin' for

When you meet that special someone
Don't let go to that person
You'll never know what to expect
Until they're not your life anymore

Spendin' all this time by myself
Is not as easy as it seems
But finding the right one
It will take more time than you think

Don't let go of me so fast
If we were meant to be together
I wanted our love to last
From now and forever

Dreamin'

If I'm dreamin'
Don't wake me up
Everything that I'm seein'
Would be hard to detect

I wasn't gonna give up on my dream
No matter what anyone say
My life isn't what it seems
I'm gonna make it big anyway

Dreamin' about you and me day and night
I'm imaginin' all the possibilities
Is what my life supposed to be
Showin' you all my abilities

Embarrassed

I feel embarrassed about all the little things
That I dunno what else to do
I dunno what my life would bring
But I still be here waitin' for you

I'm embarrassed about the way I act at times
It's better for me to get away
For the rest of my life
I don't have to be afraid

Sometimes I tend to be embarrassed
Even though I don't show it
Dunno how other's would react
To what I told them

Empty Places

I've been in these empty places for so long
I didn't know how else I was gonna go on
Even after all this time
Still I had to face everything by myself

Expect the unexpected
When I'm in these empty places
It felt kinda deceptive
In all these small spaces

With all the space in the world
I still end up in these empty places
Even if it was kinda absurd
I only can count the ways

End Of The Road

This is not the end of the road
No matter how hard things would get
It's impossible to go back
Even though I wasn't sure where I'll end up

It's a struggle but I still survive
At the end of the road there still a chance
I still believe that I can revive
Without anyone giving me another glance

If you're not in my life
What would I do now
It's the end of the road for me now
How would I move on from this now

I give and give to those who have less
This doesn't mean that we're at the end of the road
I think that this is for the best
Still I don't feel like I'm sold

Frustration

There are times that I built frustration
That I take it on others
There are times that I wanna be alone
And not be bothered

When I'm frustrated I rather be alone
Since no one really understand what I've been through
When I'm by myself at my home
I didn't think about you at all

Cannot believe this pain I'm in
All this frustration that I have inside
I thought it was gonna drive me insane
Instead of makin' me feel alive

Give Me A Reason

Give me a reason for not trusting you
Everything that you told me were all lies
How was I supposed to depend on you now
If you weren't around for me to seek the truth

I wasn't sure what to expect from you anymore
Then give me a reason for believing you now
I have to think twice before I decide anything
Since the last time I saw you around

I dunno what you expect from me
If I haven't seen you since who knows when
Why don't you give me a reason to stay
When you went away

Don't let me regret meeting you
Don't make me go back
Give me a reason for not deceiving you
And not recognizing it from the start

Grace

I'm fallin' from grace
There are little pieces of me all over the place
My life was far from over
It's not gonna get easier as I get older

I'm fallin' from grace
Within a tiny little space
Livin' in a shadow
Where it was dense and hollow

I'm fallin' from grace
When everythin' unexpectedly became a disgrace
What would I do now
Since my life was over anyhow

I'm fallin' from grace
I was hurt in so many ways
Exhilaratin' time after time
And not bein' in a bind

Happy Ending

All I want is to have a happy ending
It's what I've been wishing and hoping for
Instead of doing a little mending
Looking back for more

Happy endings don't always come around
Is what I known is what I found
I dunno where I belong
I dunno what went wrong

Getting away from all the hostility
I'm waiting for my happy ending
Thank you for giving me the ability
To do the things I enjoy and love

Thinking back what I've been through
I don't remember of one happy ending
What the world is coming to
Is this the end for all of us

Heartless

There are a lot of people who are heartless
They don't care who they hurt
People judge each other by their looks
Without getting to know one another

We forget what's important
That we don't see the person for who they are
They tend to be heartless inside
And not be considerate of others feelings

Where did we go wrong
Why do you have to be so heartless
I tried stay strong
So where has our happiness gone

Getting back to reality
I see the real you
Even if you're as heartless as the next person
It doesn't matter what other people think of you

Hurt

The only time I hurt is when you hurt
It's hard to go back and change the past
I was tryna stay alert
And not go back to that life

I was alert as I can be
It made me unaware
I didn't want you to get hurt by me
So stay away if you dare

Praying to make it right
Everything went wrong at the end
What hurts the most was that you weren't near me
I tried to do what's best for the both of us

Whenever I think back
I wonder if we can stay in touch
But it still hurts
Every time I ran out of luck

If I Could Escape

If I could escape
I would escape from all this hostility
Maybe go to a place where no one knows me

If I could escape
I'll go where I would be treated with respect
Instead of feelin' like a reject

If I could escape
I would escape to an exotic place
Where I could relax and not think about anything

If I could escape
I'll go where no one would find me
And live in peace and harmony

If I could escape
I would travel all over the world
To meet all kinds of people

I'm Lookin' For Love

I'm lookin' for love in all the wrong places
I'm lookin' for love in all the small and tight spaces
I dunno where else to look anymore
It's harder to look now more than ever before

I dunno what to do now
Till this day I still be lookin' for love anyhow
No one knows how hard I try
I try so hard and I have no reason why

I'm lookin' for love cause I don't wanna end up alone
I want cha to know that I'll be waitin' for you
What am I gonna do without you
Cause I'm still lookin' for love

Believe that I'll find you
Cause I still be lookin' for love that's true
I feel helpless when you're not around
And that's why I'm lookin' for love

I'm Real

If you get to know the real me
You'll see that I'm for real
I always try to be what others expect of me
But I wasn't sure if I was the real deal

I feel that I can be myself
Only if I got the chance
I could show you that I'm real
Without taking one glance

Being me is not as easy as it may seem
Still I try to keep it real
I'm real no matter what people think
It's just the way I feel

People have to accept me for who I am
I'm real no matter what others might say
I've been real since the beginning of time
I wasn't gonna change for anyone any time soon

In a time

In a time where the economy is changing
From one day at a time
There's not much we can do about it

We try to live the life the way we see it
Its not gonna change any time soon
In a time like this

Living in this shallow world
In a time when there's so little to give
To give to others as much as we can

Whenever society looks to get better
In a time where the economy is getting worse
Without anyone fighting together

Infidelity

Its not infidelity if it's just two friends
How is it infidelity if no one takes action
I can't believe how naïve you're being
If all I wanted was to catch up

Even though I haven't seen u for so long
It doesn't change how I feel
It didn't matter now
Since u moved on too

Couldn't understand what infidelity was
If that's not what I'm about
What were you tryna say
What was u shoutin' about

I was lookin' for a shoulder to cry on
I didn't think it was infidelity
Where our friendship has gone
And when would we get it back indefinitely

Intuition

When I followed my heart
I try to keep my intuition up
I feel like I'm drifting apart
And can't get it together

I need to trust my intuition
If not I'll fail
I had a perfect vision to look far away
Of a long trail

With every intuition I had
I don't know where my life is heading
I wasn't sure if I should be happy or sad
In this type of setting

That's why it's important to follow your intuition
Cause it takes you where you wanna go
You follow your heart every time
And make it sweet each time around

Invincible

Sometimes I feel invincible
Even though I'm not
There are times I feel invisible
So I try to give everything that I got

When I feel unbreakable
I leave little trends
When I feel invincible
It seems like my heart will mend

I'm helpless but I try holdin' on
Even if I'm invincible
The only thing that holds me back
Is not standing up for what I believe in

At times I feel weak
So how can I be invincible
It makes it harder for me to speak
That nothing would make it separable

I've Been Thinkin' About U

Even though we haven't seen each other in a long time
That doesn't mean that I've stopped thinkin' of u
I've been thinkin' about u at all the time
Wonderin' what u've been up to

I've been thinkin' about u
Since the last time we saw each other
It's been so long that is hard to remember
I'll never forget you forever

After not seein' u all these years
I wonder what u look like
Just wancha to know
That I've been thinkin' about u

It'll help me to cope
Since the last time I saw u
I've been thinkin' about u
Ever since that we first spoke

Help me to move on
It's been hard after all these years
But I've been thinkin' about u
Still tryna release my fears

Lose Me

Lose another
Lose me instead
Lose me for the better
Lose me with dignity

Lose me never
Lose me again
Lose me forever
Lose me as a friend

Lose me today
Lose me whenever
Lose me in every way
Lose me all together

Lose me if you wish
Lose if you want
Lose me without any hostility
Lose me when I'm gone

Loser

Sometimes I feel like a loser
Cause no one gives me a chance
I would like to feel like a winner
For once in my life

I believe I could thrive
And do so much more
Dunno what I should decide
So maybe I should wait a little longer

Wasn't sure where my life is headed now
But I still have high hopes
What I'm gonna do anyhow
And how am I gonna cope

I'm not gonna feel depressed
Instead I'm gonna hold my head up high
I'm not gonna think like a loser like the rest
So why don't you step out

Missing

I wasn't sure what I was missing
Until it wasn't there anymore
What needed fixing
If its not gonna be the same as it was before

What's missing in my life
Was someone special
Maybe I found him now
And I don't want to let him go

It's hard to find what I'm lookin' for
I wasn't sure what I've been missing
It wasn't the same as before
It made me realize how lucky I've been feeling

More Than Words

There are more than words that I can't handle
What can we believe if the truth doesn't come out
It's hard to determine what would happen next
If we only have one life to live

I'm sitting here all alone every day
There are more than words I can't explain
Sometimes I feel so empty inside
That there's no place to hide

I wasn't sure what lies ahead
It's never easy to deal with it
There are more than words that can't be said
I just hope that we don't end up dead

When you hesitate even for a minute
We don't think about the consequences
There are more than words that we have to learn
We have to deal with the expense

Move On

It's hard to move on
When I'm tryna hold on to u
I never expect us to meet again
But here we are one last time

I believe in the unthinkable
But it's time for me to move on
My life is sinkable
So how can I go on

I hated the way our love ended
But I need to move on
My heart needed time to mend
Even though it was so long ago

I wanted was for u to stay
But it was hard for me to hold on
When u went away
I knew it was time for me to move on

My Own Worst Enemy

I'm my own worst enemy
At times I don't know what I want
I tend to make the wrong decisions
And it never goes according to plan

I'm my own worst enemy
Sometimes I wish I was two people instead of one
Didn't know how things supposed to be done
Unless I try to do them in a different way

I'm my own worst enemy
I try to do things differently
It still doesn't seem the same
But I try my best

I'm my own worst enemy
I give up tryin' cause everything seems so hard
I try so hard but nothin' works for me
So it's better for me to let it go easily

My Reflection

Nobody sees the real me
They only see my reflection
What you really see
Is someone that is looking for attention

What you see is not what it seems
All you see is a shadow of my reflection
Asking me how things been
It was for my own redemption

Whatever happens, happens
To see my reflection once again
Tryna figure out what I was looking for
Still it wasn't the same as before

I began to realize something else
And that's something I never seen before
When I saw my own reflection on the street
It's the first time I thought about how I look

No Way Out

There's no way out of this life
There's nowhere to turn
Even if you're not by my side
What else do I have to learn

I needed to get outta this town
But there's no way out
Where would I go now
If I have no place to go

I spent so many days alone
I have no way out now
I hated waitin' by the phone
It's all I had for now

Dunno how I'm getting' outta this hole
I see that there's no way out
Instead of waitin' for someone to come home
To try to get me to stay

Nobody's Fool

Even though people play me for a fool
Still I'm nobody's fool
Either you start treatin' me right
Or I'll leave you like the fool that you are tonight

I'm always real to you
So don't play me for a fool
Cause I'm always been straight with you
You see that I'm nobody's fool

Nobody really cares to help me
So why should I try
I'm nobody's fool anymore
Then it's better for me to fly away

People say so many things about me
But they don't think before they do
That's why I'm nobody's fool
That's why I don't care about nothing now

One Wish

I only have one wish
And that's to make it big
I dunno how I'm gonna do that
But it's what I dreamed ever since I was a kid

I want to show others what I'm about
It's easy to have dreams
Still I have only one wish
And I'll do anything to make it come true

I have one wish to make
I'll do whatever I can
What does it take
To get where I plan

I look back at this time
I only had one wish
Didn't have time to unwind
I just wanted everything to be right

Only U

Only u can make me feel like a woman
Only u know me better than anyone
It's been years since we seen each other
But I still think of u

Believe that we will meet again
Only u are the one that I needed by my side
Whatever happens at the end
I'll see u on the other side

At the beginning I saw your shadow
I felt safe when I'm with u
Still only u came back to me
At the right time when I needed u the most

Begin to imagine all the possibilities
Cause only u know the right buttons to push
Only if u would have seen me in a different light
And not in a dark room all alone

Pain To Go Away

I wish this pain would go away
Instead of coming back to haunt me
It's better to wait
Wait to see how things turn out for me

When I go to that special place
I want to forget all the bad things
Wishin' that this pain would go away
Instead of makin' me feel this weak

What should I do now
If this pain is not gonna go away
Dunno where I'm going from here
Until the very next day

Remembrance

I remember every little thing about cha
Even though we haven't seen each other in a long time
I can't live without cha
I thought we were meant to be together

I remember the good times we had
It seems so long ago
I'm just glad
That everything happened the way it did

I don't remember the last time I was happy
I guess I have think back
Then I started thinkin'
About the good times we had

Safe

It's better to be safe than sorry
It's better to know what we're up against
We try to relate to those who surround us
Even though is not as easy as we thought

We make assumptions and believe everything we hear
We deal with the consequences later
How safe are we in this society
How safe are we in any society

We look back at our past
And wonder where in our lives we went wrong
We try to stay safe for our own good
And tryna stay strong

When we go out into the real world
We hope that we still be safe
As we leave the nest for the first time
We don't wanna do anything we hate

Say My Name

Say my name
Don't forget it
Cause if you do
You know you'll regret it

Say my name
Believe in what I can do
Even everything that has happened
My life won't be the same without you

Every time you say my name
Remember everything from the start
Even when nothing seems the same
Our lives won't be a world apart

I dunno what to do now
But if you say my name
I'll remember it for the rest of my life

Sense Of Insecurity

We all have a sense of insecurities
That we wonder what other people might say
We try to fit in with the cool groups
But we wonder if they will accept us
Once they actually meet us

We know who our real friends are
So there's no reason to have a sense of insecurity
Even when we see someone that we like
We're not sure if they would feel the same way

No matter what we do it's never acknowledged
We still have to believe in ourselves
We have a sense of insecurity
We're not gonna let that hold us back

It's never easy to admit being wrong
We might have a sense of insecurity
Others might think differently
But we know the truth

Single

I've been single for a very long time
Sometimes I wonder if I ever meet someone
At times it makes me think twice
About how I live my life

Being single is as hard as it is
It's not gonna get any easier
Life is what it is
And I'll never forget it

People don't wanna get to know me
That's why I'm still single
It's already hard enough to be me
When I try to stay limber

Dunno why I'm still single till this day
I probably gonna stay like that forever
What should I do anyways
If being single is not what I expected

So Small

These images of you seem so small
It's hard to see without a microscope
So why don't you let me see you in a new light
Instead of letting me wait for a long time

We crumble into little pieces
They're so small that it's hard for me to see
What's important is how we see things
That we put it into perspective

Even the biggest things look so small
We don't think about the circumstances
We look at things just the way they are
We don't expect anything of it

Given all possibilities to change your mind
You still look so small to me
You're not the same person that I knew
So what do you want me to do now

Temperature

When the temperature rises I feel like fainting
It doesn't matter how hot it might get
I still try to find a way to survive

I never like the change of the temperature
It stresses me out
What can I do about it
When nature calls

When the temperature goes down
I think about the things I can't do
It makes me wonder
About the little things I forget to do

Every thing happens when it supposed to
No matter what the temperature is
I wish it would stay how I like it
But that's never gonna happen
cause of the weather doesn't let me

The Next Big Thing

I'm the next big thing
I feel like I could do so much more
I just wanna win
Like I never have won before

I'm the next big thing
I want others to see what I can do
I don't expect everything to be the same
Even without others being so critical

I'm the next big thing
I come from those with rightness
It doesn't matter what the circumstances may be
I just wanna show everyone what I'm made of

Tragedy

Everything that has happened in the world
Has been a tragedy
There are high hopes that things will get better
But who knows what will happen tomorrow

There's always a pattern going on
It's how we deal with the circumstances
Whatever tragedy we have to deal with
We have to deal with it and move on

Without knowing all the details
I wouldn't know why good people leave us
Help me understand all the tragedies that's going on
Instead of dealing with it forever

Tragedies happens when you least expect it
I believe that sooner or later people will come together
Lately I've been thinking long and hard
About every situation that comes up
And not forget about those we're close to

True Colors

When I see your true colors
I could see right through you
When you showed me the real you
It made me think twice too

I would like to believe everything you said
But I still saw your true colors
Wasn't sure what made me feel this way
I didn't want to hold anything back

When all my feelings surfaced
It made me think about old times
As I saw the true colors coming from you
It's hard to believe in you

It's easier to follow the rules
Than to break them
Even though you couldn't see the true colors of me
It doesn't mean to I couldn't see the real you

Unbelievable

People may say that it's unbelievable what I can do
No one understood exactly what I was going through
So I had to show them what I'm about
It wasn't easy but I try my best to show you

I can't believe everything that has happened
It just seems so unbelievable what you were askin' for
I didn't get it at the beginning
But now I understand everything crystal clear

What's unbelievable is how I live my life
What I don't have is someone by my side
Now that I think of it, it still seems unbelievable
That I'm still single to this day

Unbreakable

Our love is unbreakable
Even though we are unstoppable
Why are we responsible
If we weren't even together

We were unbreakable
Even before we got together
What lies beneath us
Is something unexplainable

My heart is unbreakable
It's meant to be sealed
Dunno who's reliable
Wanted my heart to be healed

We were unbreakable when we were in school
I didn't think it mattered anymore
I thought I was a fool for falling for you
But I guess I can't change the past for sure

Unfaithful 1

You were being unfaithful to me from the start
You deceived me in every way
It torned us apart
Still you decided to stay

It's been too long since I've seen you
Since that time you were unfaithful
What am I supposed to do in the mean time
Now that we're not together anymore

Believe me that at one point at a time
You were unfaithful to me
Don't think that I'm gonna forget
It's easier to forgive than to forget

I'm scared of the way I'm being treated
Still you were unfaithful to me in every way
Didn't want to feel defeated
You're still be the one to blame

Unrealiable

You're the most unreliable person I have ever met
So why you stayed around
It was better for me to let you go
Than for me to go down

Bein' the unreliable person that you are
I didn't want to have anything to do with you
I'm not gonna be waiting for your call
Or have nothing to do with you anymore

I went to you for everything
Then I saw how unreliable you tend to be
Dunno what my life would bring
After all the things that I didn't want you to see

It was undeniable what you did to me
I knew you were unreliable since the beginning
What I wanted was to make it better
Better between us from now and forever

Ur Lost

Its ur lost that you let me go
We should've taken it slow
Instead we were outta our head
And maybe we would wind up dead

I gave it all up to be with you
It was ur lost so what you were gonna do now
I believed everything you said
So why lie to get your way

I was tryna embrace everything from the start
Even though it wasn't the same
It was ur lost so don't make it harder than it is
For whatever reason you might think

Whatever happened between us was in the past
You should have known by then it was ur lost
Giving up my dreams was hard enough
Than to pay the cost for what you did

We Belong Together

You may not know it now
But we belong together
Being the only one that knows me best
It's how I put you to the test

Where did we go wrong
How we gonna fix it
We belong together from this day forward
And no one will tear us apart

As we go on with our lives
We look back in despair
Even though I may think we belong together
It doesn't mean we have to live separately

Wonders

These are the wonders of the world
We look at the world in many different ways
We haven't been told
All the aspects that was said

We look at the end of the light
And wonder what's waiting for us
We try to reach out from afar
Holding on to each other for a long time

It doesn't seem not too long ago
The wonders of life seem so sweet
It made me feel warm inside
Without making me feel so weak

You Found Me

You found me at the right time
So don't lose me so fast
I've been tryna find a sign
But there wasn't one anywhere to be found

When you found me not so long ago
I tried to stay where I am
I couldn't imagine so
I felt like no one would give a damn

Give me a reason for not leavin'
Even after you found me
After everything you did was deceivin'
So how can I let it go so easily

You found me all alone
The last time you passed by my house
When you called me on the phone
It made me wonder what we talked about

Back & Forth

We keep going back & forth
With the same fight
We never gonna get anywhere
If we can't make it right

It's better not settling
Instead of going back & forth
We're not gonna settle it all at once
Yet we try to do our best

If only you would see
Exactly what I'm tryna show you
We don't have to go back & forth
To figure everything out

As long as I can face you
I have no reason to look back
We're going back & forth all the time
Not being able to resolve anything

Back In The Days

Back in the days everyone would say
That I always been the quiet one
Those who knows me
Would say the same thing

I haven't changed a bit
I'm still the same person
Back in the days I was tryna find out who I was
And till this day I still am

Where else would I look
It's not as simple as you think
Back in the days it seems so simple
Nowadays everything seems to get harder

I look back at my life
Only to see myself in a different light
Back in the days you would think differently
But it doesn't mean that I would reconsider

Back To Life

I would like to get back to life
Back to reality that says bring me back
Where would I go, where am I headed
Who would bring me back to life

Help me to come back
I was lost in this shadow
Bring me back to life
And never let me disappear

I have a hard time convincing others
To give me a chance of life
Who's gonna bring me back to life
And let me be the person I wanna be

It's never too late to follow my dreams
Just give me a fighting chance
Why don't you bring me back to life
And see for yourself who I really am

Blind

Only you can be this blind
I wish that you could see me in a better light
What were you thinking to find
Wasn't sure why you had to start a fight

How can you be so blind
Why do you have to make it difficult
Couldn't figure out why you were being unkind
Till you told me what was going on

Wait for the right time to tell me
Instead of hiding behind
How can you be so blind
And not see what you're doing to me

What do I have to do to show you the way
Don't act like if you're blind
You know exactly what you did
So don't deny it for the last time

Communication

Communication is the most important thing
In any type of relationship
We all have our ups and downs
But it's how we deal with what's important

Whatever happens, happens
It'll be for the best
Even though we don't have any kind of communication
But it's important to open up matter what

It's complicated, its nerve wrecking
When there's no communication
How would we find the right answers
If we don't know where to look

When we talk to one another
We wonder what we gonna say
That's why communication is a factor
And not worrying about what others might say

Cruel Intentions

You showed me no respect
All you showed was some cruel intentions
Wasn't sure why you're acting this way
I have to respect you just the way you are

You're being disrespectful
You have a lot of cruel intentions
You made me feel worthless
I never want to hear from you again

Just get away from me now
With your cruel intentions
You've been hard to handle
Ever since I met you

There's no reason to be so cruel
So leave your cruel intentions behind
Stop holding me back
And let me live my life the way I want to

Don't Be A Fool 1

Don't be a fool for not choosing me
It's the worst mistake you could ever make
You could do whatever you want
But make sure that you're making the right choice

If you think straight
You don't have to worry about a thing
Don't be a fool and do something foolish
You might regret it for the rest of your life

What do you expect from me
You should've just let me go
So don't be a fool
And leave me on the sideline

Where did you go
Why didn't you wait for me
Don't be a fool
Like you always been

Dream

I've been having the same dream over and over again
I wonder what it means
It's seems more like a nightmare
I can't even wake up from

Each and every night I dream of something different
I try to reconcile with each one
At times these dreams don't make sense
But I try to understand each one of them

Wasn't sure what the worst case scenario was
Was it a dream or something else
It's hard to determine its meaning
But I'm still looking for the right answers

What would I dream about next
No one would ever know
It's been a tough few days
But sooner or later I'll get over it

Early In The Morning

It's early in the morning
And I'm up in the crack of dawn
I have no rest at times
Cause I have to wake up early

Where has my life gone
I have to worry about everyone else
I have to wake up early in the morning
I try to do as much as I could at the same time

When will I have time for myself
I have so much to do during the day
Even if I wake up early in the morning
I still don't get work done like I tended

The night is over
The sun came up
It's early in the morning
What should I do first

Faded

My world has faded away
Wasn't sure how I was gonna get it back
Nothing made sense anymore
But I wasn't gonna give up hope
Even after what went down

Nothing good ever happens to me
That's why this life of mine has faded
It's like looking into a rear view mirror
Without the looking glass

Didn't really know what's expected of me
Didn't know anything at all
But when everything seems all faded out
Where would I turn now

Everything seems so faded
Nothing looks clear for me now
Everything was written down
Nothing makes sense to me like before

For Your Eyes Only

This is for your eyes only
To see what no one else sees
What I would like for you to do
Is to take your time and reconsider

Only if I could imagine
Everything that went down
This is for your eyes only
To see what I'm tryna show you

My heart jumped out of my chest
Just the other day
This is for your eyes only
So no one else can't know about this

Get over yourself
And stop worrying so much
This is for your eyes only
Let me know exactly what you think

Former Lover

Who knows how many former lovers I have had
I don't even remember their names
I would like to forget my past
And focus on my future

I would like to forget about my former lover
And meet someone new
It's hard to meet that one person
That makes me feel special every time

It's been a miserable time for me
It's time to get over it
My former lover would say that I'm different
Only to say the same thing about another person

I gave you my all
But you're still my former lover
Don't come to me complaining now
Cause I don't want to hearing it

Freakin' Out

I'm freakin' out
I hesitated for a second
There are so many things I can't live without
No matter how much I spend

Whenever I lose something
I tend to freak out
I lose my mind
It makes me scream and shout

I don't wanna name anyone
I would like to stop freakin' out
I just wanna have a simple life
Without getting a headache

I stare at this picture for a long time
Later I start freakin' out
I can't stop shaking
What was that about

Freedom

If only I had some freedom
I could do so much more
Even if there's not a lot to do
I just have to wait and see

The more I try to break out of this life
The harder it becomes
When I get more freedom
I would go anywhere as I please

What life would I have years from now
When will I have my freedom
I guess I have to take a vow
To live a better life from now on

I don't understand how the world works
But I don't have a lot of choices
I just would like to have some freedom
Peace and mind from now and forever

Get Over Urself

Get over urself
You're not all that
I don't care what you think
And stop over exaggerating

You're not what I expected
So why don't you get over urself
Be ready to be amazed
You gotta stop complaining

I wanted to get revenge
I didn't have any ideas yet
Get over urself
And get outta my sight

You're full of urself
Why don't you just leave me alone
Now get over urself
And leave me alone

Gone

It would have been easier
Only if you were gone
Instead of putting me through all this turmoil
So leave and don't come back

What I've been through every night
It's unexplainable
Wasn't sure if I've gone crazy
Or probably something different

What else could go wrong
What would happened once you're gone
I just have to move on with my life
I try to stay strong for my own good

Once you're gone from my life
I could focus on what I've been working for
No one said it was gonna be an easy journey
But I'll do my best without you

I Found A Place

I found a place where I feel secured
I don't wanna leave this place
Cause it means so much to me
Even if you're not here next to me

Where would I go now
Since I found a place I could call home
You left me hangin' for so long
That it was better for me to let you go

This place that I call home
It's a place that I don't wanna leave
Now that I found a place I could call my own
I never wanna leave this special place

I've been lookin' for this place for so long
I wasn't sure how I was gonna go on
I found a place where is close to heart
That I never wanna let it go

I Surrender

I surrender to you for the last time
I wasn't sure what you expect from me
I felt so self-conscious of my looks
I didn't know what else to do

With everything that's been going on
I surrender without thinking twice
It's time for me to move on
And forget about you from now on

It's never easy to look back
Even if I surrender
You should take some time
And realize what has to be done

When will I have a chance to be me
Why should I surrender to you
I never felt like if I neglected you at any time
But it won't be the last time

J Swear

I swear that my life is gonna change for the better
I wish it would be sooner than later
I would like for those close to me
To believe in me more

Only if I'm given a chance
I swear I'll show you what I'm about
Never think twice about me
Cause you know you'll regret it some day

Even when I'm alone
I feel like the walls are tumbling down
I swear my life shouldn't end this way
So what I should do differently

I look back at this time
And let it all sync in
I swear it wasn't the same
But nothing will ever gonna change

I'll Take You There

If you get lost on your way here
I'll help you find the way
I just wancha to know
That I'll take you there

When you want me to show you the way
Before gettin' lost
Just call me up
And I'll take you there

I go from one place to another
And follow each sign
So when you want me to take you somewhere
I'll take you there

Since the last time you called
I try to figure out where to go
It'll take me some time
But I'll take you there anyways

I'm Feeling You

What do you expect from me
I wish that you would've understood what I'm saying
Even with everything that you did to me
I want you to know that I'm through with you

I gave you all the chances that you deserved
Than anyone I know
Even till this day
I'm feeling you

What were you thinking about
When you made your decision
I want you to know I'm feeling you anyways
Without any inflictions

I wancha to know
That I'm feeling you
Even if you do something I don't like
It wouldn't matter to me anymore

Internal

Our love is internal
From here to there
Where ever it goes
It goes everywhere

It makes me get shivers
All over my body
This internal love that we shared
It never gonna get old

It shows you that it doesn't matter
What age you are
No matter how internal our love is
It'll never goes away

My heart beats faster
Every time I'm near you
It goes internal deep
Only when I get close to you

Internalty

Ever since I met you
I feel so close to you
It's like an internalty desire
To be with you from now and forever

Only if you take the time
To get to know me
It'll feel like internalty
Each day and night

I would like for you to take as much time
To be the person I know you can me
Why can't we be together for internalty
And not worry about anything ever again

Give me a chance please
We all need to take some time
But I still be there for you
From now to internalty

Intervention

This is an intervention
When are you gonna come clean
We can't make up our minds
About how to move on

We go on and on about little things
And not solve anything
We could have an intervention
To see where it'll leads

I don't want to get in the middle of things
I don't want to intervene
I don't care what you say
It's not gonna make me feel any better

I wanna be happy for the rest of my life
Instead of having an intervention
I dunno where I would end up
All I know is that it's not the end for me

Irresistible

You're so irresistible to me
Like no other person has
Thank you for believing in me
I'll see you on the other side

I see you looking at me
So perfectly together
I just think you're so irresistible
I can't live without you

One look at you
I knew you were irresistible to me
I took another glance at you
It didn't make me change my mind

When I see you around the corner
I can't stop staring at you
You look so irresistible
I don't wanna look at anyone else

Keeps Gettin' Better

Everything keep gettin' better
When you're around me
Once you're not near me anymore
I keep thinkin' about what should have been

Even when you're not near me
Life keeps gettin' better
Even though you may not think so
You still have to hold on a little closer

Whenever I want you close
You never are
This whirlwind of love keeps gettin' better
Every time I see you walking around my hood

Letting Go

Even though you're leaving us
I just want you to know that we be thinking of u
It's all about trust
It's all about me and you

Believe that you'll be missed when you're gone
Still we'll be thinking of you
I don't know how we can go on
Without you here from now on

I can't imagine not having you here
From now on
We still be thinking of you
And that's hard to do

We be thinking of you today
We be thinking of you tomorrow
We be thinking of you every day
We be thinking of you with pain and sorrow

Long Ago

It doesn't seem so long ago
That we first met
I wish I knew more
But for right now let's take it slow

I've been waiting for a long time
To tell you exactly how I feel
It seem so long ago
I don't remember the last time we spoke

I hope that you give me a chance
To show you who I really am
It doesn't seem so long ago
That I tried to open up to you

Only if I could get closer to you
I'll be the happiest person in the world
It looks like we waited long enough
But we still gonna be waiting here for a long time

Me & U

This is only between me & u
Nothing should interfere
Don't say yes and then change your mind
And then leave me out in the dust

What goes on between me & u
Should stay that way
No one has to know our business
So keep your mouth shut from now on

Whatever decision we make
Could affect us both
We should keep everything between me & u
And not open to everyone else

Where do we draw the line
Why everything has to be out in the open
If all secrets should stay between me & u
Then our lives would be in a better place

Never Forget Me

Even if you're not around anymore
Never forget me
I wonder what you're doing nowadays
But I have no way of knowing

Even though our lives are separated now
We still have some good memories
Please never forget me
As long as you shall live

We might not know each other that well
But never forget me
I hated to see you go
But I knew that it was for the best

We may be world apart
This is as far as we gotten
Never forget me for the rest of your life
Once you go back to your native country

Next To Me

If you would have been next to me
I would have been happier
What you meant to me
Was nothing more than destiny

Ever since you left without saying a word
I still felt your presence next to me
I needed time alone to think
About you not being there for me

Only if you would've thought about me
You still would have been standing next to me
Instead of leaving me there out in the sideline
You could've hold on to me a little longer

If you're not next to me today
I wouldn't be feeling so alone
Lately I've been sitting here in my room
Listening to these voices in my head

No More Lies

There's not gonna be no more lies between us
We always told each other the truth from the start
We've been in each others lives for a long time
It's hard to let you go

What happens between us stays between us
No more lies is gonna pass by us
We've been true to each other since the beginning
And that's never gonna change

Help me understand where you're coming from
Maybe it'll help a little
From now on there's not gonna be no more lies
There's only gonna be the truth from now on

Whenever I think about the past
I think about what we had
Even though you're not ready to tell the truth
There shouldn't be no more lies between us

Nobody's Home

When I get home late in the afternoon
Nobody's home waiting for me
It's like some emptiness inside
That needs to be healed

How am I supposed to go home
If there's nobody at home
How am I supposed to feel safe
If I have no place to call home

Where would I go now
Where would I stay
If there's nobody home
To keep me warm and sheltered

Only if I could believe every word you say
Only if I believe the rest
If nobody's home to hear me anyways
So who am I gonna depend on in my life

One More Chance

If I only had one more chance
I'll change my ways
Wasn't sure how I was gonna do that
But I have to find a way

With everything that went down
I had to recuperate
I only had one more chance
To redeem myself

The biggest aspect I had to learn
Is that everything happens for a reason
I only have one more chance
To show you the type of person I really am

I'm not going down without a fight
Even if I only had one more chance
I'll try to do my best
And try to make things right for the both of us

One Night

It only takes one night
For some good pleasure
What we see in sight
It's what you need to treasure

Give me time to react
Cause it only takes one night
What you need to tell me
It's exactly what I needed to hear

What I expect from you
Is not what you think
That one night that we shared
It would be hard to forget

When I see you around the corner
I have some insecurities
That one night that we spent together
Is one that I don't want to forget

Overprotected

I've been locked up tight for so long
I feel so overprotected
I would like to get outta here
But I have no place to go

I would like to go more places
Instead of being so overprotected
I want to be free
And live in peace and harmony

Where ever I choose to go
It's no one's business
I still feel overprotected
I rather be free

What a long road it has been
For me it hasn't been the same
What it looks like
Is me being overprotected by you

Paranoid

I need to stop being so paranoid
And think on the positive side
To become the person I wanna be
In the less time than you think

If we start acting paranoid
We're gonna drive ourselves crazy
But if we take our nice sweet time
Then we could get to know each other better

What have I become now
Since I stopped being so paranoid
Cause if I don't stop
I'll drive myself crazy every day

I can't rely on anyone anymore
That's why I'm being paranoid
But I can't stopped worryin' so much
That I didn't want it to take over my life

Passing Time

How would I be passing time by myself
Who would want to pass time with me
It's not easy for me to do
But I just have to wait for someone to answer me

The hardest thing for me to explain
Is how I feel at all times
Passing time here in this empty house
It's something that I have to think about

Getting over this tragic accident
Is how I'm passing my time
I couldn't deal with all the changes
But it's what I have to deal with

If only I would've taken my time
I would see what I supposed to see
Instead of sitting here anticipating something else
And dealing with the circumstances alone

Perfect Day

I'm waiting for the perfect day
To tell you how I feel
But the hardest thing for me to do
Was to let you know and keeping it real

The perfect day for me
Would be when I succeed
I want everyone to understand me
And believe in what I can do

The best thing that can happen to me
Is to be discovered by locals
The perfect day for me
Is when people listen to what I have to say

Run Away

At times I feel like if I need to run away
I don't do it cause I have no place to go
It doesn't matter and yet
I still have to live with the consequences

I have a reason to run away
I don't have anything to fall back on
But what I do have is a dream
A dream to make it big

Where would I go now
Where am I headed
So why run away
Why should I stay

Settlin'

It's hard to be settlin' down at a young age
But we can't help who we fall in love with
Even after our family starts meddlin'
We have no choice but to hide it

We never know how our family gonna react
When we let them know who we are interested in
Settlin' down with that special person
Makes our lives worth our while

We don't think straight at times
That we feel settlin' with that one person
We may not realize what we're doing
Until its too late to take it back

There's more that we have to see
Instead of settlin' at this moment
We still have high hopes for the future
But we don't have to decide anything any time soon

Step Up

It's time to step up to the plate
And admit the truth
You may not know what you did wrong
But it's better to hear it from me too

When you need me to be there for you
I'll step up and do the best that I can
I wasn't exactly sure what you expect from me
But I still gonna step up because I wanna do better

On the other side of the ocean
Someone is waiting for me
It doesn't matter who steps up now
Since you left me out in the cold too

It's long over do
Yet we can't go on any longer
Someone has to step up
And stay strong for the other

Still Smokin'

Even though I don't have what you're lookin' for
I'm still smokin' till this day
What you see now is not what you gonna get
But you can't imagine anything differently

Wasn't sure what's on your mind
But I can't change it
As you can see on your own
I'm still smokin' till this day

I gave up tryin' to convince you to give me a chance
It doesn't matter to me now
I still be smokin'
Even when you're not watchin'

Expect the unexpected
Is what you need to rely on
What you need to know
Is that I still be smokin' for a long time to come

Summer Time

Summer time is a season to enjoy the outdoors
It's warm and everyone's seem to be happier
When you see the flowers blooming
You know that its summer time

How else would you know if its summer time
If it's still cold outside
I'm getting tired of this weather
That at times I wish I lived elsewhere

I wish that it was summer time now
Maybe I wouldn't be as depressed
With all the snow that has fallen
There's no place to put the rest

It's March already and it still snowing
When is summer time coming
I'm ready for the warmer weather
And forget about all the snow that has fallen

Supernatural

If I had supernatural powers
I would have the ability to see the impossible
It gives me hope for the future
And makes me wanna do more

What were you thinkin' about the other day
Instead of stayin' in touch with me
If I had supernatural powers
I could see the damage that you have caused me

If I had supernatural powers
I would get people do whatever I tell them to
I'm gettin' tired of not havin' my way
Like everyone else around me

Nothin' seems to come easy for me
But if I had supernatural powers
I would change that in a New York minute
And be as happy as I can be

Tears

You'll probably never gonna see me in tears
But that doesn't mean that you will
I live my life in fear
Waiting for the right moment to let it go

All these tears that's coming down
I didn't know where it was coming from
Even when I fell down to the ground
It was like I was in another world

I've had a lot of broken hearts before
But I never gonna burst into tears
Even though I was looking for more
I've been waiting for this for years

The Eye

The eye sees everything
It doesn't lie when you look right at it
I never know when someone's lyin'
Or tellin' the truth

When you look right in the eye
It's like lookin' in the mirror
It tells you one thing
And mean another

Wherever the eye goes
It'll follow you everywhere you go
It reads people's minds
And tells you what you did wrong

There's No Need To Hurry

We've been in this road path before
Now we're at ends lookin' for more
So why don't we settle our differences
Cause there's no need to hurry anymore

We're not even close to an agreement
But I guess there's no need to hurry
We have to accept one another
And move on with our lives

What you expect me to do with our love
It's never the same as you can see
You should know from now on
That there's no need to hurry

There's no need to hurry love
It's about give and take
Don't try to change anything
Cause as you can see there's no reason to

Touched

I've been touched with what you did
What am I gonna expect to see next
It's better to leave everything the way it is
And stop complaining who's the best

Who's gonna notice anything
Who will be touched by your words
Who's gonna believe a word you say
Who's gonna be there for you anyways

It'll mean more only if you were there
I wished that you showed me that you cared
I be more touched
If you would've been more loving and caring

I look at your picture at night
It makes me get shivers
Yet I'm still touched
By the way you treated me
That it made me get quiver

What It Takes

What would it take for someone to believe in me
Would it take forever
I'll do what it takes to be who I know I could be
But its not gonna be easy

What does it take to have powers
The power to be heard
Only one person can answer that
I'm just not sure who that would be

With all the possibilities
I'm still tryna figure it out
Do I have what it takes
To be the person I wanna be

Looking back at my own life
I don't see anything different
Do I have what it takes to be popular
And be liked by those who's close to me

What's Left Of Me

What's left of me after everything that I've been through
I can't go back and change it
What I would like to figure out
Is how I'm gonna make it without any inflictions

I'm not sure where I belong
I wasn't sure what's left of me
I couldn't tell for how long
I wanted others to really see the real me

I don't have any strength left in me
There isn't much I can't do
Then what's left of me
Then how I'm gonna move on without you

When You Come To Me

When you come to me with sweet sorrow
It feels like if there's no tomorrow
I get lost in your eyes
Since their so mesmerizing

I don't wanna wait any longer
But I guess I have to
Cause when you come to me so late at night
I have to think twice every time

When you wake up on the wrong side
Says a lot about you
But when you come to me without any notice
It means that you can't live without me

Since you've been away
I've been tryin' to hold on to you
So when you come to me every night
It shows me that you never give up easily

When You Leave

When you leave today
You have to think about what you did
You may not remember
But I'm always here to remind you

Every time you change your mind
It made me wonder
So when you leave for the last time
You will reconsider taking me back

Guess there isn't much to say anymore
So leave my sight
When you leave my house for the last time
Think about every little thing that you have done

Give me time to recover
It's not as easy as it may seem
When you leave for the last time
You will remember me forever

Wide Open Spaces 1

I live in a wide open space
It feels like a close nit place
Wherever I go I never know where I will end up
Yet I still find my way back

I have high expectations
I need time to think
There are so many wide open spaces
That it'll be hard to find

I needed time alone
To think about all the possibilities
I still have this wide open space
To figure out what I want in my life

It's never too late to make up our minds
With all this wide open spaces that we have
It's like a looking glass
That lets you know the real truth

Wide Open Spaces 2

I need to have a wide open space
To do all the work I enjoy
It helps me to concentrate
Without anyone disturbing me

I would like to live in a wide open space
To run around and have some fun
I like to see the sun come out
And be happy to be alive

There are so many wide open spaces
I can't even count
It seems so amazing
How this place turned out

Give me some space to break
You have all of this wide open space
Either you share it with me
Or I'll make sure you do

Wrecked

My life has been a wreck for a long time
So what should I do for now
I've been tryna turn my life around
But it hasn't been an easy journey

You can tell that my life has been a total wreck
It looks like its been into one crash to another
When is it gonna get better
When will I get my life together

What would people say about me now
Now that I've been a wreck
I'm tryna come back from the dead
Yet it's been the opposite instead

Cheating Hearts

I don't believe in cheating hearts
It complicates things
In every other way

I don't like to be involve with anything
But you never know what's expected
That's why is better to get everything out in the open
And not hold anything back

You have to be pleased with who you're with
You don't have to have a cheating heart
Whoever you decide to be with
Has to be someone that you would be happy with

Don't feel left out
Don't be part of these cheating hearts
Don't forget what you're here for
Since you decided not to be with me

Emotions

There's so many emotions going on
Between us for a long time
We had our ups and we had our downs
Why forget about it for now

Going back in time
I think about all the emotions that was there
I turned back to you
Wondering what you had in mind

When I see you around the corner
I try to look the other way
Cause if I don't
All the emotions will come back

Show me how you feel
Show me all the emotions you have
It'll be better to get everything out in the open
And not hold anything back

Failed

I worked so hard in school
And now I have nothing to show for
I feel like if I failed in life
I can't go back to change it

I try so many different things
That I dunno what it will lead to
All I have are dreams and aspirations
But I still failed in life

One chance can change everything
I don't have to feel like a failure
Even though I failed at everything I did
It's not the end of the world

Where my life is headed now
I have no sense of direction
I failed really badly
But I keep trying to find the right place

When I make something of myself
Everyone's gonna regret the way they treated me
I might have failed today
But I'm not gonna let that get me down

Fire

There's a fire burning and it doesn't wanna go out
That no one knew what to do
I didn't want to leave that fast
But there wasn't much to do

The fire kept bursting in the air
That everyone ran for cover
The fire became so thick
No one wasn't able to see a thing

The place that I passed by
Seemed very innocent
When a fire started to break out
People started running in different directions

This world is not easy
But we do the best we can
When a fire broke out
The walls started to tumble down

Highway

Taking the highway
It's not that easy
Figuring out where to go
There are so many places
I just don't know

I live by the rules
Which I don't understand
The highway is not the best way to go
But we don't have a lot of choices

Going one way or another
It's a long road back
The highway is not the best way to go
The choices that we make could affect us

When I see the highway from afar
I wonder if I could cross over it
Due to the economic plunge
No one knows what to do anymore

I Wanna Be

I wanna be the best writer I can be
I have the heart and soul to make a difference
When you look into my eyes
You'll see right through me

After years has passed by
I know what I wanna be
That's to be the best writer
You laid eyes on

It doesn't matter what I wanna be
As long as I'm happy
You'll see a different side of me
A side you never seen before

Whatever I decide to do with my life
It's nothing out of the ordinary
I wanna be the best writer I can be
Without anyone telling me what to do

Independent

I'm a woman who's independent
That's why I don't have to answer to anyone
All the messages I'm sending
Is that I can make my own decisions

Being independent means more now than ever before
It's hard to live my life the way I see it
Even after everything that went down
Is what I would like to believe in

What's important to me is being noticed
That's what being independent is about
Especially what we have sought
I would give everything I got

Reliving all the memories at once
Didn't imagine the possibilities
Being an independent woman
Have so many responsibilities

It's Not Over

It's not over until I say it's over
Check yourself before you wreck yourself
It's never too late to start all over
So give yourself a break for once

Stop being a fool
You're just full of yourself
So when I say it's not over
Then that's what I mean

You're not the only one
Right now it's not over
You want what you want
Make sure it's what you need

I expected nothing out of the ordinary
I had to let you know that it's not over
How can I make you change your mind
Before it's too late

Not Seein' U

It kills me not seein' u
I wish things were different
Every time I pass by to see u
I hope to see u there

It breaks my heart
Not seein' u
I'm not gonna stop coming around
Till you realize that we were meant to be

Not seein' u every day
Makes me sad inside
Now that you're in my life
I don't want to let you go

What hurts the most
Is not seein' u every day
I hope that the next time I pass by
You'll be there waiting for me

Nothing But A Miracle

Every thing that I worked for
It's nothing but a miracle
It's not what I was hoping for
But I have to get over it

Even though my future is unclear right now
I'm not gonna stop excelling
Yet when you read outside the lines
You'll say it's nothing but a miracle

When there's nothing else to do
I still gonna pursue one dream
You say it's nothing but a miracle
So maybe that's how it is

What can one person say
When one person does something
It's nothing but a miracle
To accomplish ones defeat

One Call Away

I'm only one call away
I'll be waiting for your call
I wasn't sure what to say
Why don't you give me a clue

I'm waiting silently at home
To hear from you
I'm only one call away
Hoping to hear some good news

Maybe if one person cares about me
I'll wait for that moment to come
I'm only one call away
So don't hesitate to pick up the phone

Believe in the impossible
That there's no wrong answer
I'm only one call away
From making your dreams come true

One Last Time

I would like to be with you
One last time
To have some good memories
Like we had in the past

It's hard to move on
Since you're still in my life
I'm gonna tell you this one last time
That I can't be with you anymore

You might play me for a fool
This one last time
You decided not to give me a chance
So now I could move on with my life

I won't be needing you anymore
So leave my sight this one last time
I'm not gonna ask you again
To leave me alone for the last time

Piece Of Me

You know every piece of me
Like no one else
I try to open up to others
But it hasn't been easy

Only you know me better than anyone
You know every piece of me
I wonder what could have been
If you chose differently

Whatever is decided
Should be decided between us
You might know every piece of me
So why others can do the same

I wish other's see me the way you do
But no one takes the time
That's why you know every piece of me
And other's don't

Privilege

I have the privilege to do anything I want
It shows dignity and pride
It gives me the power and liberty
To make all the decisions for myself

All the things that I had planned
Wasn't what I expected
It was my privilege to make it right
For everyone in my life

I have the privilege to do what I want
Even though I wasn't sure what it was
I tried to believe everyone
But nothing seem to make sense to me anymore

I have a privilege and I tend to keep it that way
Wasn't sure what it meant
Everything that I was tryna seek
Wasn't what I tended things to go

Public Affair

It's like a public affair
Like one you never seen before
We've been here, we've been there
We've been everywhere

There's not a lot to do
But to wait for the right time
We had a public affair years ago
And its one that can't be forgotten

Whatever you think
It's not true
Even though we had a public affair
That doesn't mean that our friendship is over

Don't give up so easily
We'll meet again
When we had a public affair long ago
It doesn't mean that it's the end

Remember Me

I would like people to remember me for me
It's easier to forget about me for sure
I wanna help you see what I see
Every time you look right at me

When I'm not around it's easer to forget about me
When I try to be vulnerable
It's easier to accept me
Just the way I am

Don't expect me to run after you
But if you remember me
I'll never forget you forever

Remember me when I make it
Cause you never know what you're missing
Guess you never gonna accept it
How I decided to my live my life now

Say Somethin'

It's always better to say somethin'
Than to say nothin'
You never know what you're gettin' yourself into
Until you actually find yourself in trouble

There's not much that one person can do
Unless someone say somethin'
Once we start opening our mouth
We have to think before anythin'

Where did we go wrong
Why do you have to say somethin'
You should've kept everything to yourself
Instead of blurting out our business

It's not necessary to say somethin' you don't mean
Whatever your expectations may be
The decision that you make today
Could inflict on you later on

Surprise

It's no surprise that my life has crumbled down
I tried so hard to fit in everywhere
I haven't been able to make things right
How am I gonna fix it

Where ever I decide to go
I never know where I would end up
There's no surprise about my life
I just tryna find my own way

I needed a peace of mind
Instead of dealing with all of this frustration
So there shouldn't be a surprise
How things turned out like

It feels like hell
I don't need another surprise
I just wanna have some fun
And not worry about a thing

That's Not My Name

I heard someone calling out for me
But I wasn't sure if I heard right
So when I saw someone waving at me
I let them know that that's not my name

There's no excuse for your mistakes
You should've known my name
But when you called me from a different name
I had to let you know that that's not my name

You should think before you speak
Some people just say whatever
So why say a name that's not mine
That's why I had to let you know
That that's not my name

When you look me up on the list
Look for the right name
When you called out for me
I had to let you know that that's not my name

Everywhere I go I hear people calling for me
Wasn't sure if I heard them right
I had to remind them
That that's not my name

We have to get one thing straight
That my name is not what you think
Next time that you call out for me
I don't have to remind you
That that's not my name

The Life Of The Party

I would like to fit in the crowd
I would like to be the life of the party
There are so many people in the crowd
You never gonna find me anywhere

You'll never gonna find me in this place
I dream of being the life of the party
Give me a break for once in my life
And take the time to get to know me

I would like to be living the life
The life of the party
I wanted to see everyone close to me
Everyone that's been friends with me for a long time

The music was blasting loud
I'm just wanna be the life of the party
Only those who known me for a long time
Will remember me this one last time

Toxic

You're toxic to me
So stay away
You need to get your own life
And leave me alone

I don't understand what you tryna do to me
You're just as toxic as the next person
So stay away from me, away very far
And never look back

Give me a moment to reflect on myself
Didn't even have time to think
You're as toxic as the next person
Even though you don't realize it right away

You're just being ignorant
That's why you're toxic
I don't need to slip under
To make me feel worse than I already do

Ur Hero

All I ever wanted was to be ur hero
To be the only person in ur life
I never wanted to see you go
Even though it would have been for the last time

When you come close to me
You'll see the difference
If you let me be ur hero
You'll never regret it for once in your life

I never seen you like this before
You seem so alone and desperate
If you let me be ur hero
It would be like nothing has changed

There are times like these
That we take it for granted
But with all the circumstances
I still wanna be ur hero

Still I Rise

You can push me down
And still I rise from the ground
When you see me now
I'm more myself today without you anyhow

Pretending that everything is goin' good
You still didn't understood
Still I rise from above
And do the things that I love

You began to tell me what you wanna say
Still I rise and never go away
From time to time
My life is worth every dime

I will rise today
I will rise to stay
Still I rise before your eyes
And I will rise without your sad goodbyes

Light On

Leave the light on
For me to see
It helps me see everything in sight
Instead of looking in the dark
And giving me a fright

Everywhere I go
The light seems to be off
If the light were on
Then there wouldn't be any problems

I need to have the light on
To do everything during the day
It helps me focus
To do the things that I love to do

Whatever I have to do
I need to have the light on
No matter what I do
I never can't get any work done

Miracle

I've been waitin' for a miracle to come along
I'm hopin' that this would be the year
Didn't want anything to go wrong
So that's why I'm still standing here

Miracles happened when it supposed to
So why worry so much
When I see an angel near me
It makes me feel alive again

The important aspects is waiting around the corner
What miracles are waiting for me
Seeing everything up close and personal
Made me wonder what wasn't there at the beginning

Unfaithful 2

I couldn't understand
Why you're being unfaithful
You say one thing when you mean another
That it's hard to believe a word you say

I wish things were the same as before
But we can't change what has become
We've been on a different path in our lives
I have to respect it even though I may not like it

No one believes in every story
What else can be said that hasn't been told
When you were being unfaithful
You weren't thinking about my feelings at all

You got me tangled in your web of lies
That I can't break through
Even when you were being unfaithful
I couldn't back down at any time

Don't Be A Fool 2

Don't be a fool
You should really think about the consequences
Only if you wanted to give us another chance
And not give up so soon

If you make the right choice for yourself
You'll be surprise of what you can do
So don't be a fool
And do something you'll regret forever

Don't wait for the last minute
To make the right decision
Don't be a fool
And get over yourself for your own good

Don't be a fool
And say something you regret later
Why don't think before taking charge
That way you get all the right answers

What You Did To Me

You think you know me
But you don't
You think I'm gonna cry
But I won't

I had a whole new start
Yet you took it away from me
You made my life a living hell
That's something I'll never forget

Now that I have a whole new start
I want to forget those days
It won't be easy
Still I hold my head up high

I never forget what you did to me
But I'll move on with my life
It's the only way
I could live the way I want

So Far Away

You seem so far away
That I can barely touch you
Even though we never met
That doesn't mean that I'm not thinking about you

We lost contact for a period of time
But we're back in each other's lives now
I wondered what you looked like
I left that a mystery

Holding on to that memory
Seemed so hard to do
I left that memory behind
Even if you were so far away

Waiting for a response from you
Seems like forever
Still I'm waiting patiently
And it's not for the better

You Being In My Life

We started talking to each other long time ago
Yet it seems like yesterday
I still think about you every now and then
Wondering if you think about me too

Over the years I read the letter you sent to me
I felt so close to you
Wishing that you were near me
Instead of a world apart

My life feels so empty without you
Yet when you were in my life
At least I had a purpose
A purpose to do anything I put my mind to

You were like an incomplete dream
Still you being in my life
It made me feel like I'm the only girl in the world
Who had everything to live for

You Stayed

Even though we're miles apart
I'm glad that you stayed close
We never know what could've been
So we have to wait till that day

Since the day we started chatting
I wonder where we would end up
Its 10 years later and you still in my life
Which is more than most people ever known

So many people have come and gone
Yet you are the one who stayed
Even when you moved away
You stayed close in my heart

We didn't speak for years
I wondered how you were
You stayed in my life
Even when no one else did

Deaf & Blind

I wish I was deaf
I wish I was blind
Cause everywhere I go
People treat me so unkind

Even if people acts nicely
I rather not to listen
I would like to be deaf & blind
That way I don't hear what others say

Being deaf & blind
Is not as bad as you think
Cause not hearing what others say about me
Will make me feel even worst

Being Around You

I known you forever
Still you're a mystery
I try my best to be around you
But lately you been unavailable

I dunno where our lives would end up
But still I'm tryna get to know you
I guess there are others more important than me
How can I compete

I wish I was number one on your list
But I'm not even close
How you think that makes me feel
That there are others more important them me

Call Me

I wish that you would call me
I missed hearing your voice
I tried so hard seeing you
But you never around

I never met anyone like you before
I don't wanna lose you again
My heart beats faster every time I think of you
It makes me realize how short life is

My life feels empty without you
I wish that you would call me
I can't make you do something you don't wanna do
No matter what the circumstances may be

I'll be waiting for your call
So call me whenever you can
We'll be having a ball together
In any type of weather

Lost & Found

I once was lost
Let me show you how it really went down
Like the thought of you of being real
Knowing what its worth was the real deal

The latest news was not confirmed
It's what I thought but it was never unlearned
I came back that day to show you the way
Is what I found out the very next day

You played me like a fool
I knew it wasn't cool
Seeing you looking fine
But baby you know my name is divine

Feeling the life and feeling the thirst
I knew it was taken a turn for the worst
So step out you fool
And don't come back cause it's not cool